Lexcel Financial Management and Business Planning Toolkit

Related titles from Law Society Publishing:

Lexcel Business Continuity Planning Toolkit
The Law Society

Lexcel Client Care Toolkit (2nd edn)
The Law Society

Lexcel Information Management Toolkit
The Law Society

Lexcel People Management Toolkit
The Law Society

Lexcel Risk Management Toolkit
The Law Society

All books from Law Society Publishing can be ordered through good bookshops or direct from our distributors, Prolog, by telephone 0870 850 1422 or e-mail **lawsociety@prolog.uk.com**. Please confirm the price before ordering.

For further information or a catalogue, please contact our editorial and marketing office by e-mail **publishing@lawsociety.org.uk**.

Equality and Diversity in Practice

These online training courses, which take account of the provisions of the Equality Act 2010, can be taken as a combined package (£85 for 2.5 hours' CPD) or individually:

- **Equality and Diversity Essentials:** an introduction to the concepts of equal opportunities and diversity and an overview of the legislation (£50 for 1.5 hour's CPD).
- **Managing Diversity:** how managers and supervisors can comply with discrimination legislation and manage diverse teams effectively (£45 for 1 hour's CPD).

See **www.lawsociety.org.uk/cpdcentre**.

Lexcel Financial Management and Business Planning Toolkit

The Law Society

The Law Society

ISBN 978-1-85328-746-6

Published in 2011 by the Law Society
113 Chancery Lane, London WC2A 1PL

Typeset by Columns Design XML Ltd, Reading
Printed by Hobbs the Printers Ltd, Totton, Hants

The paper used for the text pages of this book is FSC certified. FSC (the Forest Stewardship Council) is an international network to promote responsible management of the world's forests.

Contents

Preface

Law firms and in-house legal departments alike will continue to face increasing economic pressures and greater demands from clients within a changing legal landscape. Having effective management systems embedded in your practice will help you to survive. Business planning and financial management must be developed, maintained and reviewed regularly by any practice wanting to be successful.

In particular, the Legal Services Act 2007, in force from October 2011, will have a varied impact on practices. Increased competition may be caused, for example, by the launch of alternative business structures (ABSs) and the advent of well-known brands entering the legal services market. Firms who anticipate that this will generate additional competition should already be looking at their business and financial plans to review the impact on their practice. By reviewing their plans before the Act comes into force, firms will be able to better assess the potential impact and implement effective solutions to support their business post-October.

Alternatively, if you are a firm interested in external investment, mergers or takeovers, consider the impact of having well thought-through business plans and financial information – the better you present yourself, the more attractive you will be. If you are considering merging, you should be looking to develop a partnership with an organisation that has effective planning and financial management systems already in place.

Another consideration is that to meet the Solicitors Regulation Authority's information-gathering requirements, practices will need to evaluate their systems and ensure they implement support for data provision. Effective financial management systems will be particularly important for these requirements. Preparing early on and ensuring you have access to relevant information will make dealing with the changes easier.

Business and financial plans are core elements to success. They will assist practices in identifying business-critical objectives and working out how to fulfil them within their own environment. As with all effective management strategies, transparency, communication and review processes are important to successfully obtaining these objectives. Having supportive and rigorous systems in place will also help mitigate risks that may affect the implementation and success of any plans.

The *Lexcel Financial Management and Business Planning Toolkit* is designed to provide an outline of best practice approaches and templates to adapt and implement within your practice. Practices wanting to use the templates need to review and amend them to ensure that what they implement is truly relevant for their practice.

We would like to thank Andrew Otterburn for contributing to the financial management sections of this Toolkit and the Institute of Legal Finance and Management (**www.ilfm.org.uk**) (formerly the Institute of Legal Cashiers and Administrators) for allowing us to use material from their Associate course in this publication.

Lexcel Office
The Law Society

1 Business planning

1.1 The Lexcel requirements

Lexcel v4.1 has the following requirement:

2 Strategic plans

2.1 Practices will develop and maintain a marketing and business plan that includes measurable objectives for the next 12 months, which must include:

(a) the person responsible for the plan
(b) a procedure for a review of the plan to be conducted every six months to verify the plan is in effective operation across the practice.

2.2 Practices will document the services they wish to offer, including:

(a) the client groups to be served
(b) how services are to be provided
(c) a procedure for a review of services to be conducted every six months.

2 Preparing for business planning

2.1   Why use a business plan?

Every practice wanting to maximise its performance needs an objective and robust business plan. Regularly reviewed to enhance relevancy, the plan must be understood and supported across the organisation. In particular, it must be driven and endorsed by the senior management team. Practices with effective management frameworks will have business planning as an integral part of their business. Such plans will be especially important for law firms as the full implications of the Legal Services Act 2007 start to become apparent when it comes into force in October 2011.

Business strategies are a key part of business planning. If a practice lacks strategic plans, it is harder to manage and more likely to fail. Each practice's business plan will be different due to the nature of individual organisations.

A template business plan is included in **Appendix 2A**.

2.2   In-house legal department plans

As an in-house legal department you may have organisation-wide business plans and reviews, but you should also have a practice-specific plan that is more relevant to, and truly reflects, your department. Of course, any department-specific plan must also feed in to and complement the organisation-wide plan. In addition, as a core part of the business, legal departments will provide essential support to enable the business to work towards and achieve its objectives. Being more involved in the wider organisation's business planning process can help identify and mitigate risks which may affect one or multiple areas of the business.

2.3   Sensitivity of plans

Business plans are an important part of communicating key information about the practice to its staff. Within the plan, however, there may be sensitive elements that should not be shared within the practice. For example, if a practice's plan includes details of potential staff redundancies later in the year, management may deem it unsuitable for all employees to know these details. In such cases, a brief version of the business plan could be produced which excludes the sensitive details but still provides the essential direction to help steer the practice.

2.4   Timescales and reviews

Business plans should be produced annually and synchronised with a practice's financial year. This will help with financial management, objective setting and result collation and review.

Irrespective of the type or size of practice, business plans should be reviewed on a regular basis and involve at least everyone within the senior management team. To comply with the Lexcel standard, practices must review their plans every six months. In times of increased competition, economic challenge or regulatory change, practices should consider more frequent reviews in order to maximise the relevancy of their plans.

2.5   More than one plan

Most practices are likely to find it useful to create more than one business plan. This is often the case where there is one overarching plan that instigates the creation of several or many more plans, for example, in a practice where there is more than one practice area, multiple teams or various office sites. The creation of such focused plans increases the relevance of the plans to different areas within the organisation and enables more focused objectives, targets, monitoring of results and risk identification. In practices where they exist, any focused plans must still support the larger organisation-wide plan.

2.6   Top-down or bottom-up planning

The direction of business planning can be top down or bottom up. This relates to where the detail for the plan is driven from. Ideally, a combination should be used, where senior management provide overarching strategy, objectives and targets, and managers within the organisation provide the detail that will support them.

2.7   Planning preparation

2.7.1   Review your situation

Reviewing your current business plan can be a highly effective starting point. It can help to focus minds and makes use of recent experience and knowledge to develop the plan for the year ahead. Remember that one of the most valuable parts of the process is discussion and debate. The final document merely summarises what has been agreed; the real value lies in the discussions along the way.

The review should include looking for trends in:

- Summaries of your accounts over the last 12 months and, if applicable, the last three years, including fees, salaries, overheads, borrowings, debtors and work in progress.
- Summaries of fees by work type and client over the last three years.
- Market changes, including geographical spread and demographics where possible.
- Market indicators from organisations that may impact on your work levels.

Practices should consider conducting a 'SWOT' analysis where you identify strengths, weaknesses, opportunities and threats (see **Appendix 2B** for SWOT analysis grid). Alternatively (or as a complementary exercise), a 'PESTLE' analysis could be performed in which you assess political, economic, social, technological, environmental and legal factors that might impact on the practice (see **Appendix 2C**). The idea behind both is to identify and evaluate issues that might potentially impact on your practice.

2.7.2 Get feedback

Consider obtaining input from all practice staff as well as from managers. This could produce useful feedback and valuable ideas for inclusion in the plan or its development.

You can obtain input in a variety of ways, for example, one-to-one, team or department meetings, or by means of a questionnaire. An example of a staff feedback questionnaire is included in **Appendix 2D**. When selecting a feedback method, practices should think about which option is the best both for obtaining the type of information wanted and for staff.

The perceived confidentiality of a questionnaire could affect results as staff may feel uncomfortable giving feedback directly. If this is a concern, consider circulating a questionnaire that can be completed anonymously or having an external person collate the feedback. Staff may feel more at ease if their responses cannot be linked to them.

As well as asking staff, it is possible to learn a considerable amount from clients and professional contacts. Asking contacts can sometimes be of greater value than asking clients as they are often better able to compare your practice with other solicitors.

Section 7 of the Lexcel standard requires practices to have a procedure to monitor client satisfaction, and for many practices this might include a client satisfaction survey (a pro forma is included in the *Lexcel Client Care Toolkit*). If it is completed effectively, such a survey may provide valuable insight into how the practice, its services and market are perceived, and how client service could be improved.

> Discussing how you can better help them achieve their objectives and the level and type of service they want from you is not remotely unprofessional – if you fail to do so your client is likely to stop instructing you.
>
> Heather Stewart, *Client Service for Law Firms*, Law Society 2011

2.8 Think about key milestones

The business plan must include key milestones – critical actions required at certain points in time. The Lexcel standard indicates that the plan must include measurable objectives for the next 12 months. It may be difficult to have many action points more than six months in the future, but try to predict further into the year. Thinking about key actions now may clarify planning in the longer term or help mitigate risks. Practices should include milestone information wherever possible in their business plan documentation.

2.9 Considerations

When preparing to plan and produce a business plan, practices need to allow for the following:

- Succession planning – this may affect the planning process, for example, if a key member of the planning team is leaving the organisation.
- Lack of money for investment – may hinder plans.
- Lack of leadership or an unwillingness by management to be led – could make it difficult to obtain sign-off or commitment from management.
- Lack of a shared vision amongst the management team – could impact on timescales for producing the draft or even final plan.
- An inability to plan – lack of skills, experience and authority could result in an ineffective process or irrelevant plan.
- Lack of information – if data such as financial information is hard to obtain or inaccurate, the quality of the plan will be compromised.

2.10 Project management

Planning a business plan is a project in its own right and must be given serious consideration. A project plan will help clarify timescales, responsibilities and the process to anyone involved in the business plan's creation, development, revision or approval.

Business planning should be carried out by someone with suitable experience, skills and authority within the practice.

Timelines for producing a project plan will vary dependent on the size and complexity of a practice. Practices should allow at least four weeks to write, review and finalise the plan. In more complex practices, it will take longer. In either case, a realistic target should be set in advance and the plan should not be left until the last minute.

The project plan should include the following information about the business plan:

- Author – the name and position of the person responsible for producing the plan. Make sure they have the relevant experience, skills and authority.
- Approver/sponsor – the person who will sign off the plan, typically a member of the senior management team.
- Reviewer(s) – name(s) of any colleagues responsible for reviewing the plan. Typically, this will be the senior management team.
  Contributors – these are often partners, heads of department or managers with responsibility for budgets, products/services or support services within the practice (e.g. human resources, finance, IT, procurement and facilities).
- Plan creation date.
- Plan version – this will ensure the most up-to-date version is being used.
- Objectives – high-level objectives for the plan.
- Budget – any costs associated with the delivery of the business plan.
- Targets – specific targets for the project, which could simply be the completion date of the business plan.
- Risks – any risks that may affect whether the project achieves its objectives or outcomes.
- Project plan timeline – an overview of key milestones and respective timescales.
- Recommendations – any recommendations the author wishes to put forward to the reviewer(s) or sponsor.
- Clarification of terms – make sure the plan is easy to understand and not overly complex.

A basic project plan template is provided in **Appendix 2E**.

3 The business plan

3.1 Author(s) and contributor(s)

3.1.1 Author(s)

The business plan author needs to have suitable experience, skills and authority within the practice. There may be one or multiple plan authors within a practice. A plan author should be responsible for:

- co-ordinating all the information for their plan;
- collating all the information for their plan;
- completing the business plan template using the information supplied from colleagues;
- meeting with other plan authors to discuss economies of scale or duplication of activities;
- communicating and sharing versions of their plan with relevant colleagues so that they can contribute;
- working with the leaders of support services, such as finance and human resources, to ensure the business plan and budgets are aligned.

A business plan author should *not*:

- write the business plan in isolation;
- write the plan information from scratch – much of it should already exist.

3.1.2 Contributors

As mentioned above, the author will not write the business plan in isolation – other people will contribute to it. Contributors are often partners, heads of department or managers with responsibility for budgets, products/services or support services within the practice (e.g. human resources, finance, IT, procurement and facilities).

3.2 Approver or sponsor

The approver or sponsor is the person responsible for overall approval and sign-off of the plan. At practice level this is usually the managing or senior partner, or head of legal for in-house departments. For business plans produced at department or team level, the sponsor may be the leader of the department or team.

3.3   Date and version

During the business planning process and as a result of reviews, details of the business plan may change. Including the date and version will ensure colleagues refer to the most up-to-date version of the plan.

3.4   Objectives

The practice's objectives must be developed to truly reflect the strategy for the next 12 months. There should be no more than 10 objectives in the practice-level business plan. By including more than this, the practice will risk having objectives that are irrelevant, unsuitable and less specific. The objectives must be measurable – details of how the success of the objectives will be measured should be outlined in the key performance indicators (KPIs) for the practice.

3.5   Key performance indicators

KPIs are measures that focus on those aspects of organisational performance that are most critical for the current and future success of the organisation. They can be financial or non-financial measures. Department- or team-level KPIs should link to the overall organisation-level KPIs. A KPI should:

- be able to be measured frequently;
- be acted on by CEO and senior management;
- be understood by all staff, including any corrective action required if the KPI is not met;
- tie responsibility to the individual and/or team;
- have a significant and positive impact.

Examples of KPIs are given at **Appendix 3A**.

3.6   Budget overview

An overview of the practice's high-level budget should be included in the plan to provide a clear parameter for everyone within the organisation. The details can vary but should cover all key account or cost codes for expenditure and income. If sensitivity is an issue, practices may consider opting for a short paragraph outline rather than figures. Bear in mind, though, that managers within the practice will likely hold responsibility for their own budgets, so visibility of the budget should be shared with them. In particular, during times of change, providing an overview may help cement any alterations for the practice or particular areas within it.

3.7   Resources

The resources section of your business plan should outline current staffing levels and types across the entire practice. It should be provided in numerical and graphical form (e.g. an organisation chart) to provide clarity and ensure your starting point is accurate. The figures and structure may change during the 12 months so it is important to update these details during reviews. This will be particularly useful if the practice changes as it will help keep people up to date and provide a transparent outline of the business.

3.8   Product(s) and/or service(s) offered

3.8.1   Current offering

Most business plans will include details of target client groups and the services to be offered. The Lexcel standard requires that this information is documented. The Lexcel standard also requires that this information is made clear to clients and other people such as potential referrers of work, for example, on the practice's website.

During the preparation stage of business planning, the practice should have reviewed and agreed any changes to their product or service offering. The information in this section should, therefore, confirm these plans and so cover existing and new offerings for the next 12 months.

A lot can happen in 12 months, however, e.g. mergers. Practices should update their offering details as part of the review process at the least, or consider doing so more frequently as and when new offerings are identified and investigated.

More complex practices should consider including details of offerings by practice area, department and team. Setting out this information clearly within the business plan can provide a useful overview of the practice's structure. For both law firms and in-house legal departments, an outline of products and services can also be a highly effective way of increasing awareness of the offerings to existing and potential clients, and can be used to identify and promote internal and external cross-marketing and selling.

Practices may also want to consider carrying out further analysis of their products and services, such as a SWOT and/or a PESTLE analysis (see **Appendices 2B** and **2C**).

3.8.2   Product/service development

New products or services to be launched in the next 12 months should be included in the business plan. This will help ensure that the right levels of financial and staff resources, amongst other requirements, are planned for if not estimated. Failure to include these details in the plan may significantly impact end-of-year performance results.

3.9   Clients and markets

Both law firms and in-house legal departments should know who their client(s) and target audience(s) are. For an in-house legal department, this may be specific teams or individuals within the organisation. Law firms will have primarily external clients, from consumers to organisations. Taking time to identify current service buyers and potential targets can result in more effective targeting of activities. The business plan should, therefore, include an overview of current clients and their use of your offerings.

Ideally, client or market analysis should be presented in both numerical and graphical format; the latter often helps people visualise differences or key points. It will be essential to work with colleagues to generate this data. For example, colleagues with responsibilities for IT (in particular, a customer relationship management system or a case management tool) or financial management should be able to provide relevant statistics such as fees per client.

The more analysis you conduct, the more likely you are to maximise your knowledge of your offerings and clients, as well the potential effectiveness of your marketing activities in the next 12 months. Questions to ask when developing your business plan should include:

*   What is our market place and who are our clients?
*   How is our market changing?
*   Where do we see ourselves in these markets – now and in the future?
*   What are our goals with regard to specific clients or markets?

A more detailed list of questions that could be asked is included at **Appendix 3B**.

3.10   Business development and marketing

The terms 'business development' and 'marketing' are easily interchangeable in some practices. Historically, business development has implied more focus on tenders, client-focused activities and lead generation in a more target-driven way. Marketing can, however, cover the same areas and should use the same detail- and results-orientated methods to support the practice. However they are defined, business development and marketing for the next 12 months will be an essential part of your practice's business plan.

This section will be of use to in-house legal departments and private practices, as both should focus on direct and indirect promotion of the practice to fulfil its objectives. For example, some in-house legal departments who gain Lexcel accreditation hold an event to promote the achievement within the department and the organisation, and invite senior management colleagues.

Business development and marketing are, however, areas in which law firms invest more heavily, with specific and sometimes substantial budgets and resources allocated to this function of the business. Where dedicated resources are invested in business development or marketing, a separate plan should be produced to detail activities for the next 12 months.

Conducting the pre-business plan review, as outlined previously, should inform your decisions in terms of planning business development and marketing. At a basic level, marketing should focus on the '4 Ps':

- Product – what it is you are offering
- Price – cost to produce and market to client
- Promotion – how, when and where it will be promoted
- Place – where it will be obtained

In general, business development or marketing plans should cover:

- Proposal documentation
- Fact-sheets, brochures and other collateral material
- Direct mail (electronic and hard copy), including announcements, magazines and newsletters
- Events, including client events, receptions, seminars and speaking engagements
- Public relations
- Advertising – internal and external
- Internet presence – the practice's own website and external websites
- Branding
- Thought leadership – where staff are positioned as experts or leaders within the market

The business development and marketing plans within your practice-level business plan can be high level to ensure a general awareness of activities, resources, responsibilities and timescales. The business development and marketing section can include a table providing the following details per main activity:

- Objective – what the practice seeks to achieve
- Brief description – overview of what the activity is
- KPIs – targets and measures
- Budget – expenditure and income (actual and estimated)
- Timescales – when the activity will take place
- Responsibility – who will deliver the activity
- Activity outlines – what will be delivered in the next 12 months

It is recommended that separate plan(s) be produced to cover business development and marketing, especially for more complex or larger organisations. Separate plan(s) will enable more detail to be included for all activities. A basic template marketing plan is included in **Appendix 3C**.

3.11   Operational infrastructure

A practice's operational infrastructure relates to the functions carried out by its human resources, finance, IT and facilities teams or departments.

Practices face challenges to their operational infrastructure for various reasons, for example, as a result of consolidation of legal departments within local authorities, or mergers between firms. How this affects the structure can depend on the type of change.

3.11.1 Organic growth

Arguably the best way for any practice to grow is through the selective recruitment of individual people to fill gaps and to allow for the expansion of the practice in line with its overall strategy and the opportunities available to it.

Organic growth has a number of advantages, such as:

- It is easier to retain the culture of your practice and its values. In particular, if you recruit people as trainees and train them in your ways and to your standards, it is much easier to maintain the ethos and culture of your practice.
- It is relatively easy to manage. Slow, gradual growth is generally easily absorbed within a practice and does not create serious problems for management. This is not the case, of course, if a practice is recruiting a number of people simultaneously, although such rapid expansion tends to happen in larger practices that are better able to deal with it.

It also has some disadvantages, such as:

- It is slow – if you are a small practice you might be able to accommodate recruiting an additional fee earner each year, perhaps two. At the same time your larger rivals have added 10 fee earners, perhaps 20.
- There is a real danger that, having invested time and energy training someone, they are poached by another practice and you lose them just as they are becoming valuable fee earners – in particular your good people.

3.11.2 Merger

Some mergers are actually more realistically takeovers where one practice is looking to expand (perhaps through necessity) and another practice is willing to be taken over. Advantages of a genuine merger can include:

- The overnight creation of a much larger practice. For example, combine two practices each with 30 fee earners and you are suddenly a major law firm in your town, or a major in-house legal team within your area.
- The opportunity for raising the market profile of the combined practice.
- The creation of relatively strong teams from previously weak ones.

- The opportunity for managers to retire – not everyone will want to be a part of the new practice.
- In law firms, the opportunity to re-evaluate the role of equity partners – some former equity partners may become salaried in the combined practice.
- It provides a springboard for expansion.

A genuine merger can, however, have some downsides, such as:

- Someone needs to take the lead – any organisation that lacks effective leadership is likely to struggle. A merger may start out as a merger of equals, but someone needs to take a leadership role.
- Combining two small practices with poor gearing and low profits may result in a larger practice with poor gearing and low profits. Unless the opportunity is taken to change the financial structure of the combined practice, little will have been gained.
- It may be difficult to merge the two cultures. Even where two practices merge into the same building, there may be 'rival camps' several years later, in particular amongst support staff. The situation is especially difficult if staff retain the pay and conditions they had in the previous practices so that, in the combined practice, staff of the same level are not remunerated in the same way.
- There may be duplication of offices, or buildings in locations you do not see as part of your long-term strategy.
- Unless it is agreed that some departments or fee earners will not be included in the merger, you might end up with fee earners and departments you do not want. You might have been attracted by the other practice's litigation team, but you might also acquire a legal aid department that does not fit.
- IT and telecommunications systems may be incompatible. There can be a temptation to continue parallel systems for a period, which can be confusing and disruptive, and there is always a risk of argument as to which practice's systems should prevail.

3.11.3 Acquisition or takeover – of a whole practice or just a team

For a practice acquiring another practice, or another team, there are relatively few negative impacts. As indicated earlier, there are likely to be relatively few genuine mergers between two equal practices. Most mergers are, in reality, takeovers. The advantages of growth through acquisition or takeover for the acquiring practice arc:

- The same overnight creation of a much larger practice as in a merger.
- You retain your culture and standards – they are not diluted or compromised.
- If you take over just a team or department, you obtain only the people you want.
- If you take over a whole practice, you are in a strong position to address performance issues.

- It will be much easier to integrate the new people into your systems. Unless the target practice's systems are better, you should be able to introduce your IT systems and ways of working relatively easily.
- It is much easier to improve the financial structure.

The advantages for the practice being acquired (the target practice) are:

- It can provide senior management with an exit route.
- The management of the practice is now in someone else's hands.
- The fee earners, in particular the more recently qualified, may have a wider range of career possibilities.

The main disadvantages are:

- Management in the target practice may have inflated the performance of their business which will require scrutiny once staff have transitioned into the new organisation.
- The target practice's partners may feel vulnerable to unfair treatment after they have signed away their independence. There will need to be a well thought-through agreement that protects their position.
- Management might find it difficult to be managed – they are used to being the main decision takers in their former practice and it will probably feel extremely strange to be managed by someone else.
- Some staff may have difficulty accepting new working conditions and practices. Long-serving, and therefore probably valuable, staff may struggle in the new environment and leave.

3.11.4 The best option?

Arguably there is no ideal scenario and the needs of each practice will differ. Factors to take into consideration are a practice's:

- leadership;
- management structure and framework;
- clarity of business strategy;
- financial awareness;
- quality of client service;
- reputation and market share;
- compliance and claims history;
- internal culture;
- business development and marketing;
- internal support services and infrastructure, including human resources and IT.

3.12   Risks

The Lexcel standard requires:

> 1.2 Practices will have a risk management policy, which must include:
>
> (a)   strategic risk
> (b)   operational risk
> (c)   regulatory risk
> (d)   the person responsible for the policy
> (e)   a procedure for an annual review of the policy, to verify it is in effective operation across the practice.

Meeting these requirements should provide any practice with a good foundation for identifying and managing risks for their practice. These risks should be considered prior to drafting the business plan. In particular, a practice's risk register should be referred to during business planning as the register will provide details of specific risks facing the practice.

Within the business plan, it may be useful to insert a table with information about the risks including:

- Risk reference – there are likely to be multiple risks so a reference can aid identification
- Owner – person with responsibility for the risk
- Manager – person with responsibility for managing the risk
- Description – brief outline of the risk
- Risk rating and probability – level and likelihood of risk
- Key actions – actions required to mitigate or manage risk

For more information on risk management, refer to the *Lexcel Risk Management Guide* available from the Lexcel office (e-mail: **lexcel@lawsociety.org.uk**) or the *Lexcel Risk Management Toolkit* available from the Law Society bookshop (**www. lawsociety.org.uk/bookshop**).

3.13   Policy statements

3.13.1 Equality and diversity statement and corporate responsibility statement

Practices should include their equality and diversity statement and corporate social responsibility statement in their business plan. Doing so reinforces the practice's commitment to these principles and ensures they are considered in every activity the practice undertakes. Examples of equality and diversity statements can be found in **Appendix 3D.**

3.13.2 Equality Impact Assessment

An Equality Impact Assessment (EIA) provides the opportunity to review the business plan objectives and proposed activities and assess whether they are likely to have an impact (either positive or negative) on a particular group of people, for example, in terms of age (older or younger people), gender, disability, race, sexual orientation, or religion or belief. Information about the EIA process is provided in **Appendix 3E**.

For more information on equality and diversity and corporate social responsibility within the legal profession, visit the Law Society website: **www.lawsociety.org.uk/ inclusioncharter**.

3.14   Recommendations

The business plan should include any recommendations the plan author wishes to put forward to the reviewer(s) or approver/sponsor.

4 Financial management

4.1 The Lexcel requirements

3   Financial management

3.1 Practices will document responsibility for overall financial management.

3.2 Practices will be able to provide documentary evidence of their financial management processes, including:

(a)   annual budget (including, where appropriate, any capital expenditure proposed)
(b)   variance analysis conducted at least quarterly of income and expenditure against budgets
(c)   annual profit and loss or income and expenditure accounts
(d)   annual balance sheet
(e)   annual cash or funds flow forecast to be reviewed quarterly
(f)   quarterly variance analysis which includes at least their cash flow

3.3 Practices will have a time recording process which enables the accurate measurement of time spent on matters for billing purposes.

3.4 Practices will have a procedure in relation to billing clients, including:

(a)   the frequency and terms for billing clients
(b)   credit limits for new and existing clients
(c)   the person responsible for the procedures
(d)   a documented review of the procedures at least annually, to verify they are in effective operation across the practice.

3.5 Practices will have a procedure for the handling of financial transactions including:

(a)   the person responsible for the procedures
(b)   a documented review of the procedures at least annually, to verify they are in effective operation across the practice.

The whole section is mandatory. Well-managed practices are likely to be complying with most if not all of these requirements.

4.2   Responsibility for financial management

As part of a practice's management arrangements, it is important that it is clear who is responsible for financial management. For law firms this has traditionally been a partner; increasingly, however, particularly in larger practices, it is a finance director. Since the introduction of non-lawyer partners in 2009, this person can actually also be a partner or member in the practice. For in-house practices, the person responsible for financial management of the legal department may be someone within the team, or be a colleague in the organisation's finance department. In-house practices should ensure this responsibility is confirmed and communicated to ensure compliance with internal and external requirements.

For any type of practice, the responsibility for day-to-day financial management may be vested in a finance manager or cashier. If this is the case, an organisation chart that indicates who is responsible for what will be very useful.

Wherever the person responsible for financial management resides or whatever their job title, they must have all the relevant qualifications, experience, skills and authority to effectively manage your practice's finances.

With the introduction of ABSs from October 2011, the SRA will require practices to have a Head of Finance and Administration. Practices should start investigating who would a suitable person for this role to ensure compliance from that date.

4.3   Budgets

To meet requirement 3.2 of the Lexcel standard, practices need to demonstrate that they comply with six specific six areas of financial management. They do not need documented procedures in respect of these; however, there must be documentary evidence that the practice has financial management processes in place.

The first financial management area concerns budgets. Budgets are an essential tool in the financial management of any practice. They provide an opportunity to outline plans for the coming year, which can then be measured against actual results. This chapter describes the most typical methods of preparing a budget.

4.4   Preparing the budget

The best time to prepare a budget is in the last two months of the financial year, when the outcome for the year can be predicted with a degree of certainty. This is normally when practices update their business plans, so preparing budgets at the same time complements the process.

Preparing the budget is in fact an essential part of preparing the business plan. The budget outlines finances and financial management requirements, and if the financial information does not support the business plan, it can lead to a re-working of the plan.

A budget is normally for 12 months, to the end of the next financial year. Some practices do, however, extend it in outline for a further two years. Practices should consider the most suitable timescale for their practice and implement what they deem is best. At the least, though, it should be for a 12-month period.

A practice's accountant or cashier would normally prepare the budget, but department heads, team leaders and fee earners should also be involved. It is not hard to prepare and need not take long, but you need to keep it simple!

4.5 Starting point

There are many ways to prepare a budget. In essence, you have to take a view of the practice's anticipated income and expenditure. What should not happen is for one person to try to determine the budget on his or her own without discussion with those with responsibility to deliver against it.

It is always much easier to forecast what the practice's expenditure is going to be than forecast its income. This is because most expenditure is based on regular outgoings. For example, the current cost for employing a five-person team can be calculated relatively easily. Expenditure is, therefore, often a good place to start.

The largest items of expenditure for most practices are going to be:

- salaries (together with employers' national insurance contributions (NIC) and pensions);
- rent and rates;
- professional indemnity insurance (PII).

For some practices, notably criminal law practices, PII might be a very low figure. For most practices, however, it is a substantial amount, sometimes on a par with rent and rates. Budgeting for PII costs can be made easier with regular communication with your PII insurer and broker, as and when factors affect your practice. In addition, costs can be known prior to the cut-off date for renewal of PII if preparation for your renewal starts well in advance of the October deadline.

The salaries budget is normally quite straightforward. The starting point is the current staff list and their existing salaries, then adjust this for any projected new staff and leavers. Practices will also need to allow for any planned pay rises and employee benefits.

Table 4.1 is for a sole practitioner with two employed solicitors and two paralegals.

Table 4.1 Salaries budget for year ending 31 March [*year*]

Name/position	Current salary (£)
Solicitor 1	45,000
Solicitor 2	35,000
Solicitor 3	25,000
Paralegal 1	15,000
Paralegal 2	15,000
Cashier	15,000
Reception	15,000
Secretary x 3	45,000
	210,000
Allowance for salary reviews (1 October) – 5% for 6 months	5,250
Planned new solicitor (from 1 October) – £25,000 for 6 months	12,500
	227,750
NIC (say 10%)	22,775
	250,525

In order to work out a monthly or quarterly budget you could simply divide this annual total by 12 or 4, to give roughly £20,900 a month or £62,700 a quarter. As both the salary reviews and the new starter are scheduled to take place on 1 October, you could use a more accurate monthly amount of £19,250 in the first six months (£210,000 ÷ 2 = £105,000 + 10% = £115,500 ÷ 6), and £22,500 in the second six months (£210,000 ÷ 2 = £105,000 + £5,250 + £12,500 = £122,750 + 10% = £135,025 ÷ 6).

When working out an expenditure budget, some professionals simply take the previous year's actual/projected figure and add a percentage for inflation. If you are preparing the budget in the last two months of the year it is certainly useful to take the forecast for the current year as a starting point. It is better to use the budget as an opportunity to challenge and question, particularly when it comes to the procurement of products and services. When preparing a budget, questions to consider should include:

- Why is the money being spent?
- Is the product or service essential to our practice?
- Is there an alternative product, service or supplier?
- Are we getting real value for money?

Practices should review costs in this way every year. If this is not feasible, practices should conduct a thorough review once every two or three years. An exception is PII, where the question of whether the practice is getting value for money and whether it is using the best supplier does not really arise because you have no choice. For some other items, it should also be possible to work out a budget quite quickly for next year based on the past year by taking into account any changes, for example, to the amount of floor area occupied.

For most other items it is necessary to critically evaluate the expenditure. Concentrate first on the biggest items and ask whether it is possible to buy the same quality and quantity but at a lower price. Areas such as auditing and accountancy, insurance and stationery could be periodically reviewed and perhaps put out to tender as part of this process. Car schemes for partners and senior staff have been another area where some practices have been able to achieve significant savings.

A very useful approach which some practices use is known as 'zero based budgeting' whereby they start with a zero budget for each item and then justify each pound spent. This can work well in areas such as marketing, library services and training. Departmental heads could be asked to list the books they need or the courses they want to send staff on. This is an approach that everyone can understand and that can be monitored.

It can also be useful to split the practice's expenditure by specific departments or teams, particularly if you want to produce departmental accounts and therefore need to be able to set departmental budgets.

4.6 Types of expenditure

Expenditure items at practice level should include:

- rent and rates;
- heating and light;
- PII and other insurance;
- depreciation;
- postage;
- telephone;
- photocopying;
- stationery;
- general library;
- general marketing/business development;
- general training;
- human resources;
- IT;
- finance;
- facilities;
- procurement.

Departmental overheads could include:

- departmental marketing/business development;
- training;
- unbilled disbursements;
- old bills written off;
- department-specific library.

4.7   Overall versus department owned

Although this is a good way of making departmental managers more financially responsible, in practice charging against a department can be difficult. Individual items need to be considered and charged either to a department or centrally, depending on the objectives and targets of specific activities. Alternatively, consideration should be given as to whether fee earners in a department have to bear the cost of a bad debt incurred by previous fee earners, perhaps some time ago. Having decided which items are to be charged centrally and which are to be charged to individual departments, it should be possible to forecast some of the biggest central expenditure such as rent and service charges, rates, PII and depreciation quite quickly.

4.8   Prioritisation

In building up a budget for a particular heading you may wish to give specific items of expenditure a priority as in Table 4.2.

Table 4.2 Expenditure priority scale

Scale number	Description
1	Required urgently
2	Required within 12 months
3	Nice to have
4	Contingency

4.9   Fees

As discussed earlier, it is relatively easy to fix the salaries and overhead budgets; the more difficult area is income – the fees budget. In practice this is not normally as hard as it may first appear; it is generally relatively easy to come up with a fees budget that makes sense.

It is important to note that the fees budget is not the same as the fees target. The fees target is the figure you discuss with the fee earners and that you expect them to achieve. The fees budget may well be based upon this, but is more cautious and includes an allowance for work levels being less than expected and any difficulty in charging the fee levels you may wish. It is a more prudent figure, one you may show your bank.

For example, the three partners in Table 4.3 know they need to generate fees of approximately £750,000 in order to produce a profit of £85,000 each.

Table 4.3 Budget for year ending 31 March [*year*]

	(£)
Salaries	250,000
Overheads	245,000
Profit required for the partner to achieve post tax and pensions drawings of £4,000 a month – say, £85,000 x 3	255,000
	750,000

It can be useful to work out the fees that should be generated by each fee earner by looking at the previous two or three years, as in Table 4.4.

Table 4.4 Fees generated by each fee earner

Fee earner	Fees earned for year ended 31 March (£)		
	XXX0	XXX1	XXX2
Partner 1	100,000	140,000	150,000
Partner 2	110,000	115,000	120,000
Partner 3	90,000	105,000	115,000
Solicitor 1	60,000	70,000	85,000
Solicitor 2	50,000	60,000	70,000
Solicitor 3	40,000	50,000	60,000
Paralegal 1	10,000	30,000	40,000
Paralegal 2	10,000	30,000	40,000
	470,000	600,000	680,000

If your practice bills on a time basis it might be possible to also work out a fees budget based on the number of chargeable hours each fee earner produces and their hourly rate as in Table 4.5.

Table 4.5 Fees budget for year ending 31 March [*year*]

Fee earner	Assumed annual chargeable hours	Hourly rate (£)	Income (£)
Partner 1	1,000	140	140,000
Partner 2	1,000	140	140,000
Partner 3	1,000	140	140,000
Solicitor 1	1,000	100	100,000
Solicitor 2	1,000	100	100,000
Solicitor 3	1,000	100	100,000
Paralegal 1	800	60	48,000
Paralegal 2	800	60	48,000
New solicitor	400	100	40,000
Fees target			856,000
Contingency – say 12.5%			107,000
Fees budget			**749,000**

If your practice does not bill on a time basis it should be possible to complete a similar schedule based upon the number of each type of matter you expect to complete multiplied by the rate you are paid for each type.

4.10   Final profit and loss budget

The final budget, based upon fees of £750,000 and also including an estimate for interest received is summarised in Table 4.6.

Table 4.6   Budget for year ending 31 March [*year*]

		(£)
Fees		750,000
Interest		10,000
		760,000
Salaries		250,000
Overheads		
Rent and rates	75,000	
Heating and light	15,000	
PII	40,000	
Other insurance	13,000	
Auditing and accountancy	12,000	

Cleaning	2,000	
Depreciation	15,000	
Postage	5,000	
Telephone	18,000	
Photocopying	2,000	
Stationery	6,000	
Marketing	2,000	
Training	4,000	
Library	15,000	
Sundries	15,000	
Recruitment	1,000	
Costs draughtsman	5,000	245,000
Net profit		**265,000**

A monthly or quarterly budget would normally be obtained by dividing these annual totals by 12 or 4 for certain items. If practices can phase the budget more accurately based on seasonal trends in fees, they should try to do this. In addition, for certain items, such as marketing, budgets can be set by month as activities can be planned in advance.

4.11 Capital expenditure budget

In addition to the budget, which indicates the profit or loss the practice is projected to achieve, it is important to prepare a capital expenditure budget.

Once again this is not necessarily complicated, as in Table 4.7.

Table 4.7 Capital expenditure budget for year ending 31 March [*year*]

		(£)
Office alterations		55,000
IT – new PCs	25,000	
– new server	15,000	40,000
		95,000

Consideration will also need to be given as to whether this will be paid in cash or funded through leasing or some other form of finance.

4.12 Summary

This chapter has described, using fairly simple examples, how a practice might prepare a budget – both a profit and loss budget and a capital expenditure budget. Having a well thought-through budget, linked to the practice's business strategy, is a key starting point for effective financial management, and a Lexcel requirement.

5 Variance analysis

Once practices have set a budget, the Lexcel standard (at 3.2(b)) requires them to monitor their actual performance against this budget on a regular basis – at least quarterly. The principal reason for producing management accounts is to help assess your practice's results for the year so far. They are normally at the heart of a practice's management.

It is important to devise a format for management accounts that focuses on the key figures and provides information that is easy to understand. The accounts need to be prepared quickly after the period end while it is still fresh in people's minds, and as accurately as possible. Some practices produce accounts monthly, but others find an in-depth review on a quarterly basis works better. The important point is that the accounts are looked at and action taken if necessary.

Traditionally, practices produced a set of management accounts based on the format of their annual accounts as shown in Table 5.1. Many practices continue to do this, and indeed the format set out in this table would comply with the Lexcel standard.

Table 5.1 Smith & Co. – Accounts – Period 8 – November

(£)	This period		Year to date	
	Budget	Actual	Budget	Actual
Fees	250,000	235,458	2,000,000	1,850,478
Interest receivable	2,000	1,758	16,000	14,569
	252,000	237,216	2,016,000	1,865,047
Salaries	95,000	96,785	760,000	775,852
Rent and rates	12,500	12,658	100,000	102,457
Light and heat	3,000	2,480	24,000	18,456
Telephone	5,000	3,254	40,000	36,741
Printing, stationery	4,500	5,521	36,000	29,963
Postage and DX	2,000	2,321	16,000	16,879
PII	6,000	6,000	48,000	48,000
Other insurance	1,800	1,700	14,400	13,789
Repairs	2,000	1,563	16,000	13,258
Accountancy	1,500	1,500	12,000	12,000
Subscriptions	2,000	1,850	16,000	14,785
Library	2,000	2,245	16,000	14,587

(£)	This period		Year to date	
	Budget	Actual	Budget	Actual
Training	2,000	2,203	16,000	14,695
Marketing	2,000	1,756	16,000	17,458
Depreciation	7,500	7,500	60,000	60,000
Bad debts	2,000	1,458	16,000	14,789
Cleaning	750	745	6,000	5,895
Miscellaneous	3,000	2,896	24,000	22,458
Negligence claims	4,000	2,147	32,000	26,789
Bank charges	1,500	1,452	12,000	11,478
Bank interest	2,000	2,851	16,000	17,452
Motor and travel	1,800	2,504	14,400	17,825
Annuities (previous partners)	3,000	3,000	24,000	24,000
Practising certificates	2,500	2,500	20,000	20,000
	169,350	168,889	1,354,800	1,349,606
Profit	82,650	68,327	661,200	515,441

Drawbacks of this format, which is probably used by 75 per cent of practices, include:

- The numbers, because they are expressed in single pounds, are difficult to read. A potential improvement would be for them to be expressed in £'000s or to three significant digits, i.e. 237 instead of 237,216.
- It is difficult to identify trends because the partners would be given a new set of accounts for each month.
- Too much emphasis is placed on overheads, which in many practices are often close to budget.
- There is insufficient analysis of fees and gross profit.

Table 5.2 presents the same information in a very different format. These accounts are for November, which is mid-way through the third quarter. The first two quarters are shown in total and the actual results are shown for the first two months of this quarter together with a projection for December.

In this report less emphasis is placed on overheads – which are shown as just one line – and there is greater emphasis on the fees earned by the five departments. This highlights straightaway where the problems lie, as well as the fact that some departments are actually ahead of budget.

Table 5.3 shows the same format but including notional salaries for the equity partners, and is starting to show a much more useful set of figures.

Table 5.2 Smith & Co. – Accounts – Period 8 – November

(£'000)	Quarter 1 March–June Budget	Quarter 1 March–June Actual	Quarter 2 July–September Budget	Quarter 2 July–September Actual	Quarter 3 October–December October actual	November actual	December revised	Total revised	Original budget	Year to date actual	Full year projection revised	Full year original budget
Company commercial	250	220	250	126	86	79	65	230	250	511	796	1,000
Property	150	140	150	125	41	38	35	114	150	344	479	600
Employment	50	60	50	55	18	21	20	59	50	154	224	200
Litigation	200	210	200	212	72	68	70	210	200	562	832	800
Private client	100	105	100	110	35	29	30	94	100	279	409	400
Total fees	750	735	750	628	252	235	220	707	750	1,850	2,740	3,000
Interest	6	7	6	5	1	2	2	5	6	15	22	24
	756	742	756	633	253	237	222	712	756	1,865	2,762	3,024
Salaries and overheads	507	492	507	511	177	169	150	496	507	1,349	1,949	2,028
Profit	**249**	**250**	**249**	**122**	**76**	**68**	**72**	**216**	**249**	**516**	**813**	**996**

Table 5.3 Smith & Co. – Accounts – Period 8 – November (including notional salaries)

(£'000)	Quarter 1 March–June		Quarter 2 July–September		Quarter 3 October–December					Year to date actual	Full year projection revised	Full year original budget
	Budget	Actual	Budget	Actual	October actual	November actual	December revised	Total revised	Original budget			
Company commercial	250	220	250	126	86	79	65	230	250	511	796	1,000
Property	150	140	150	125	41	38	35	114	150	344	479	600
Employment	50	60	50	55	18	21	20	59	50	154	224	200
Litigation	200	210	200	212	72	68	70	210	200	562	832	800
Private client	100	105	100	110	35	29	30	94	100	279	409	400
Total fees	**750**	**735**	**750**	**628**	**252**	**235**	**220**	**707**	**750**	**1,850**	**2,740**	**3,000**
Interest	6	7	6	5	1	2	2	5	6	15	22	24
	756	**742**	**756**	**633**	**253**	**237**	**222**	**712**	**756**	**1,865**	**2,762**	**3,024**
Salaries	285	289	285	291	99	97	75	271	285	776	1,076	1,140
Notional salaries	80	80	80	80	27	27	26	80	80	214	320	320
Gross profit	**365**	**369**	**365**	**371**	**126**	**124**	**101**	**351**	**365**	**990**	**1,396**	**1,460**
Gross profit percentage	**52**	**51**	**52**	**42**	**50**	**48**	**55**	**51**	**52**	**47**	**50**	**52**
Overheads	222	203	222	220	78	72	75	225	222	573	873	888
Profit	**169**	**170**	**169**	**42**	**49**	**41**	**46**	**136**	**169**	**302**	**493**	**676**

5.1   Summary

Having established a budget, it is clearly very important to monitor performance on a regular basis. There will be some figures that are monitored daily, such as the bank balance, others that are produced weekly, such as chargeable hours or fees, and finally some, such as overall or departmental profitability, that can be reviewed on a monthly or quarterly basis. The key points are to design a format that people understand and to take action on the figures.

6 Cash flow forecasts

The final requirements in 3.2 of the Lexcel standard deal with cash – the need to forecast the organisation's cash flow and to monitor actual cash flow against this forecast. A profit and loss (P&L) budget, as discussed in Chapter 4, indicates the profit (or loss) you expect to make. A cash flow projection indicates the resulting bank balance this will produce. In preparing it you need to adjust for:

- non-cash items such as depreciation and any profit/loss on disposal of an asset;
- non-P&L items such as drawings, introduction and withdrawal of capital, and capital expenditure.

6.1   Depreciation

Depreciation is something many people struggle to understand. The main question is usually: Why does an adjustment have to be made?

The starting point in understanding depreciation is to think about the difference between an asset such as a computer and a consumable item such as stationery. The former, known as a fixed asset, will be used for several years whereas the latter will not – it is a consumable item that is used quickly.

A fixed asset is shown in the fixed assets column on the balance sheet, and an amount is charged each year to the P&L account in order to write it off over its life. For example, a new computer system may cost £100,000 and be expected to have a five-year life, resulting in a P&L charge of £20,000 a year – this is called depreciation.

The reason we need to adjust for depreciation in a cash flow projection is that it does not result in a movement of cash this year – the impact on cash of the purchase occurred in the year of purchase. If your starting point is your budget for the coming year, and if that budget includes a figure for depreciation, you need to adjust for it.

6.2   A simple cash flow

A simple cash flow projection is shown in Table 6.1.

Table 6.1 Cash flow for year ending 31 March XXX3

	(£)
Incomings	
Fees	750,000
Interest	10,000
	760,000
Outgoings	
Salaries & NIC	250,000
Overheads	245,000
Adjustment for depreciation	−15,000
Partner's drawings	144,000
Tax and partner's pension contribution	111,000
Capital expenditure – office alterations	55,000
Capital expenditure – IT	40,000
	830,000
Net movement	**−70,000**
Opening balance – 1 April XXX2	−100,000
Closing balance – 31 March XXX3	−170,000

Assumptions:

- Opening and closing WIP the same
- Opening and closing debtors the same
- All figures exclude VAT therefore no VAT payment shown

This cash flow forecast, albeit very simple, highlights that although the budget is indicating a profit of £265,000, more than sufficient to meet management's income expectations of £85,000 each, the overdraft is likely to nearly double as a result of capital expenditure.

The change in cash is summarised in Table 6.2.

Table 6.2 Analysis of cash movement

	(£)
Capital expenditure	−95,000
Add back depreciation	15,000
Retained profits (£265,000 less drawings and tax of £255,000)	11,000
	−70,000

The implication of this is that the management team may have to reduce their drawings, or the practice may have to negotiate an increased overdraft or loan in respect of the expenditure. The intention may have been to pay for them with cash.

In order to make practical use of this cash flow projection, you should split it into a quarterly or even monthly basis. Generally, you would phase the various figures evenly unless there were good reasons to do otherwise. Senior employees' tax is often a big figure and this is due on 31 January and 31 July, so this is worth reflecting in the appropriate quarter. In Table 6.3 the capital expenditure is all scheduled for the first quarter of the year.

Table 6.3   Cash flow for year ending 31 March XXX3

(£)	April–June	July–Sept	Oct–Dec	Jan–Mar	Year
Incomings					
Fees	187,500	187,500	187,500	187,500	750,000
Interest	2,500	2,500	2,500	2,500	10,000
	190,000	190,000	190,000	190,000	760,000
Outgoings					
Salaries and NIC	62,500	62,500	62,500	62,500	250,000
Overheads	61,250	61,250	61,250	61,250	245,000
Adjustment for depreciation	–3,750	–3,750	–3,750	–3,750	–15,000
Partner's drawings	36,000	36,000	36,000	36,000	144,000
Tax and partners' pension contribution		55,500		55,500	111,000
Capital expenditure – office alterations		55,000			55,000
Capital expenditure – IT				40,000	40,000
	156,000	266,500	156,000	251,500	830,000
Net movement	**34,000**	**–76,500**	**34,000**	**61,500**	**–70,000**
Opening balance – 1 April XXX2	–100,000	–66,000	–142,500	–108,500	–100,000
Closing balance – 31 March XXX3	–66,000	–142,500	–108,500	–170,000	–170,000

As a result of this more detailed analysis, the timing of the increased overdraft can be assessed, providing a more comprehensive picture to take to the bank. One option to consider is to lease the capital expenditure or obtain long-term funding rather than outright purchase, as this would have a big impact on the overdraft.

This method provides an overall indication of what the practice's borrowings are likely to be. If you want to monitor the actual cash flow against this projection you will need to incorporate VAT.

6.3   A more comprehensive approach – incorporating VAT

The main limitation with the approach above is that it ignores VAT, and in practice the quarterly VAT payment can be a significant amount that causes considerable cash flow difficulty. We need to build VAT into the quarterly cash flow projection prepared previously, as in Table 6.4.

Table 6.4   Cash flow for year ending 31 March XXX3

(£)	April–June	July–Sept	Oct–Dec	Jan–Mar	Year
Incomings					
Fees	187,500	187,500	187,500	187,500	750,000
Interest	2,500	2,500	2,500	2,500	10,000
Output VAT (Note 1)	37,500	37,500	37,500	37,500	150,000
	227,500	227,500	227,500	227,500	910,000
Outgoings					
Salaries and NIC	62,500	62,500	62,500	62,500	250,000
Overheads	61,250	61,250	61,250	61,250	245,000
Adjustment for depreciation	–3,750	–3,750	–3,750	–3,750	–15,000
Partners' drawings	36,000	36,000	36,000	36,000	144,000
Tax and partners' pension contribution		55,500		55,500	111,000
Capital expenditure – alterations		55,000			55,000
Capital expenditure – IT				40,000	40,000
Input VAT (Note 2)	11,500	22,500	11,500	19,500	65,000
VAT payments (Notes 3 and 4)	20,000	26,000	15,000	26,000	87,000
	187,000	315,000	182,500	297,000	982,000
Net movement	**40,000**	**-87,500**	**45,000**	**-69,500**	**–72,000**
Opening balance – 1 April XXX2	–100,000	–60,000	–147,500	–102,500	–100,000
Closing balance – 31 March XXX3	–60,000	–147,500	–102,500	–172,000	–172,000

Notes:

1. Output VAT is calculated by taking fees and multiplying by 20%
2. Input tax is calculated at 20% of all VATable inputs. It is assumed that all overheads are VATable, and that the capital expenditure is also. In practice you may decide to separate overheads into those that are VATable and those that are not – but beware of making this too complex!
3. It is assumed that the VAT quarters are June, September, December and March, with payment the following month.
4. Opening VAT credit assumed at £20,000.

VAT workings:

B/F	−20,000	−26,000	−15,000	−26,000	−20,000
Output	−37,500	−37,500	−37,000	−37,500	−150,000
Input	11,500	22,500	11,500	19,500	65,000
Payments	20,000	26,000	15,000	26,000	87,000
C/F	−26,000	−15,000	−26,000	−18,000	−18,000

This is a more meaningful cash flow projection because it is closer to reality. The projected overdraft is actually lower than in the simplified projection. It is £2,000 lower and this represents the increase in the amount of unpaid VAT – VAT which has been collected from clients, but by the year end has not been paid over to HM Revenue & Customs.

A cash flow report for the first quarter is shown in Table 6.5.

Table 6.5 Cash flow – 30 June XXX3

(£)	April–June Budget	Actual	Variance
Incomings			
Fees	187,500	160,215	−27,285
Interest	2,500	1,289	−1,211
Output VAT	37,500	32,043	−5,457
	227,500	193,547	−33,953
Outgoings			
Salaries and NIC	62,500	62,854	−354
Overheads	61,250	63,478	−2,228
Adjustment for depreciation	−3,750	−3,750	0
Partners' drawings	36,000	36,000	0
Tax and partners' pension contribution			
Capital expenditure – alterations			
Capital expenditure – IT			

(£)	April–June Budget	Actual	Variance
Input VAT	11,500	11,946	–446
VAT payments	20,000	20,000	0
	187,500	190,528	–3,028
Net movement	**40,000**	**3,019**	**–36,981**
Opening balance – 1 April XXX2	–100,000	–100,000	
Closing balance – 31 March XXX3	–60,000	–96,981	
VAT workings:			
B/F	–20,000	–20,000	
Output	–37,500	–32,043	
Input	11,500	11,946	
Payments	20,000	20,000	
C/F	–26,000	–20,097	

Note: Table 6.5, for simplicity, shows the amounts excluding VAT. It is perfectly acceptable (and much easier) to use VAT inclusive figures.

In the event, cash collection during the first quarter was £27,285 worse than anticipated, and overheads were over £2,000 higher than expected, resulting in an overdraft of £96,981 which is nearly £37,000 worse than expected.

6.4   Summary

Businesses fail due to lack of cash not lack of profit, hence the requirement in the Lexcel standard to prepare cash forecasts and update them at least quarterly during the year. After about six months it will often be useful to prepare fresh forecasts.

7 Annual accounts

Requirement 3.2 of the Lexcel standard asks for certain annual reports. This is a straightforward requirement for a practice of solicitors as the annual accounts will contain a profit and loss account and a balance sheet.

An in-house legal department should have little difficulty in producing an income and expenditure report for the year; indeed, one should be available as a matter of routine. It might be more difficult extracting a balance sheet as it is likely that one would simply be produced for the authority or company as a whole. However, it should be possible to construct something that indicates the amounts owed to and by the department, its work in progress and any bank balances.

8 Time recording

The Lexcel standard at 3.3 requires practices to have a process in respect of time recording. The standard does not require practices to have a documented procedure in respect of time recording. It will, however, generally be good practice to do so as otherwise there is likely to be inconsistency between fee earners.

The standard only requires practices to have a time recording process that enables the accurate measurement of time spent on matters for billing purposes. Many practices, however, will wish to have a process that also allows them to assess the cost of undertaking a matter and to measure fee earner productivity. In such cases it is important that both chargeable and non-chargeable time is recorded.

9 Procedures for billing clients

The Lexcel standard at 3.4 requires practices to have procedures for billing clients – key procedures both in order to ensure the practice is paid promptly and also to ensure clients are billed in accordance with the practice's client care procedures. In preparing these billing procedures, organisations will also need to be aware of the requirements in the Lexcel standard regarding client care.

10 Procedures for handling financial transactions

The Lexcel standard at 3.5 requires practices to document their procedures for handling financial transactions. The actual procedures required will depend on the organisation, but are likely to include:

- receipts of money;
- cheque payments;
- payments out of client monies;
- petty cash;
- payments to third parties such as Counsel.

APPENDIX 2A

Business plan template

[*Year*] business plan

Author: [*name of person responsible for producing the plan*]

Approver: [*name of person responsible for final review and sign-off*]

Reviewer: [*names of any colleagues responsible for reviewing the plan*]

Contributors: [*names of any colleagues contributing to the production of the plan*]

Date: [*date*]

Version: v[*number*]

Contents

1   Objectives

The high level objectives for [*name of practice/unit/department/team*] for [*year*] are:

2   Key performance indicators (KPIs)

KPI	Target	Owner

3   Budget

Expenditure is budgeted at £[*value*]. Income has been targeted at £[*value*]. Please see Annex A for the [*year*] budget for [*name of practice/unit/department/team*].

4   Resources

Overview

[*Name of practice/unit/department/team*] currently employs [*number*] permanent and [*number*] temporary staff. We currently have [*number*] [teams/departments/ practice areas] within our remit. An outline of our [practice/unit/department/team] structure and breakdown of staff can be found in Annex B.

Factors affecting resources

[*Outline factors*]

5   Products and services

[Product/service 1]

[*Outline of product/service*]

[Product/service 2]

[*Outline of product/service*]

[Product/service 3]

[*Outline of product/service*]

6   Clients and market

Client segmentation

[*Outline, including graphical representations where possible*]

Market forces and adoption

[*Outline, including graphical representations where possible*]

7   Business development and marketing

Budget

The business development/marketing budget for [*name of practice/unit/department/team*] for [*year*] is £[*value*].

Targets

Our key marketing audiences for [*year*] are:

• [*Audience*]

Overall management

[*Outline*]

Team and individual responsibilities

[*Outline*]

Lead generation

[*Outline*]

Campaign focuses

• **Topics** – [*outline*]
• **Audience segments** – [*outline*]
• **Geographic targets** – [*outline*]
• **Product/service launches** – [*outline*]

Activities

Promotional activities for [*name of practice/unit/department/team*] in [*year*] will include:

- Materials – [*outline*]
- Events – [*outline*]
- Publications – [*outline*]
- PR – [*outline*]
- Direct mail – [*outline*]
- Advertising – [*outline*]
- Cross-marketing – [*outline*]
- [Practice/department] website(s) – [*outline*]
- External website(s) – [*outline*]

8   Operational infrastructure

Human resources

[*Outline, including graphical representations where possible*]

Finance

[*Outline, including graphical representations where possible*]

IT

[*Outline, including graphical representations where possible*]

Facilities

[*Outline, including graphical representations where possible*]

9   Risks

Regulatory

[*Outline*]

Strategic

[*Outline*]

Operational

[*Outline*]

Financial

[*Outline*]

Competition/reputational

[*Outline*]

Technological

[*Outline*]

10 Policy statements

Equality and diversity statement

[*Practice's equality and diversity statement*]

Corporate and social responsibility statement

[*Practice's corporate and social responsibility statement*]

11 Recommendations

[Recommendation heading]

[*Outline*]

Annex A: [name of practice/unit/department/team] budget

[Year] budget
Cost centre: [reference]
Project reference: [reference]

		J	F	M	A	M	J	J	A	S	O	N	D	Year budget	Year actual	Variance
Income																
[Item code]	Fees													£0	£0	£0
[Item code]	Interest													£0	£0	£0
[Item code]	Course and function income													£0	£0	£0
[Item code]	Commission/licence income													£0	£0	£0
[Item code]	Sponsorship income													£0	£0	£0
[Item code]	Sundry income													£0	£0	£0
Total income		£0	£0	£0	£0	£0	£0	£0	£0	£0	£0	£0	£0	£0	£0	£0
Staff expenditure																
[Item code]	Basic salaries													£0	£0	£0
[Item code]	NIC													£0	£0	£0
[Item code]	Agency staff													£0	£0	£0
[Item code]	Medical insurance													£0	£0	£0
[Item code]	Employee benefit costs													£0	£0	£0
Non-staff expenditure																
[Item code]	Stationery supplies													£0	£0	£0
[Item code]	External printing and duplicating services													£0	£0	£0
[Item code]	Telecommunication costs													£0	£0	£0
[Item code]	Document exchange payment													£0	£0	£0

[Year] budget

Cost centre: [reference]

Project reference: [reference]

[Item code]	Postage							£0	£0	£0
[Item code]	Courier service							£0	£0	£0
[Item code]	Internal meetings							£0	£0	£0
[Item code]	Staff accommodation/meals and subsistence							£0	£0	£0
[Item code]	Taxis and car hire							£0	£0	£0
[Item code]	Non-employee expenses							£0	£0	£0
[Item code]	Conferences, exhibitions and room hire							£0	£0	£0
[Item code]	Consultancy and services							£0	£0	£0
[Item code]	Conference fees							£0	£0	£0
[Item code]	Business development/marketing							£0	£0	£0
[Item code]	Sundry expenses							£0	£0	£0
[Item code]	Books							£0	£0	£0
[Item code]	Audio visual materials/equipment							£0	£0	£0
[Item code]	Doubtful debts provision movement							£0	£0	£0
Total expenditure	£0	£0	£0	£0	£0	£0	£0	£0	£0	£0
Total net position	£0	£0	£0	£0	£0	£0	£0	£0	£0	£0

Annex B: [*name of practice/unit/department/team*] structure

[*Insert organisation chart(s) or tables – example below*]

Job title	[Unit/department/team]	Quantity	Main role responsibilities

APPENDIX 2B

SWOT analysis

Internal factors	Strengths	Weaknesses
	Highly motivated staff	Outdated IT systems
	Marketing strategy	Insufficient investment in management training
	High levels of technical competence among fee earners	Poor cash flow
	Financial reserves	High overheads
	Reputation	Ineffective performance measurement and review
External factors	Opportunities	Threats
	Alternative business structures	Alternative business structures
	Ageing population	Flat housing market
	Wills and probate work	Competition from other practices
	Acquisition or merger	E-law
	Re-mortgage and repossession work	Bank lending restrictions
	Outcomes-focused regulation	Public sector funding cuts

PESTLE analysis – examples of factors

Political

- Stability of government
- Attitude to public and private sectors
- Attitude to external regulation
- Attitude to the professional sector
- Influence of UK regions
- Increase in global interactions
- Integration with Europe

Economic

- Current economic performance
- Long-term economy
- Business performance
- Government policies
- Fiscal policies
- Interest rates
- EU influence
- Global influence
- IT impact
- Current public perception of services
- Skills shortages

Social

- Gap between rich and poor
- Shift in work patterns
- More working women
- Familiarity with IT
- Increase in direct purchases
- Increase in consumerism
- Increase in location independence
- Decline in job security
- Increase in number of self-employed
- Increase in cars/leisure time
- Increase in divorced/single parents
- Decline in school leavers
- Increase in higher education

- Social diversity
- Ageing population

Technological

- Increasing speed of change
- Increase in dependence
- Worldwide access
- Speed of access/business response
- Improved/cheaper communications
- Reducing costs
- Impact on way of working/skills shift
- Skills shortages
- 24-hour access
- Impact on accessing products/services

Legal

- Volume of legislation
- Complexity of legislation
- Increase in layers of influences – regional, national, Europe, global
- Increase in consumerism
- Increase in public access to information
- Increase in sophistication of clients

Environmental

- Increasing emphasis in business context
- Increasing legislation
- Decline in quality of environment
- Pressure on finite resources
- Potential climate change
- Increase in importance of water
- Increase in demands for energy

Staff feedback questionnaire

1 What are the best things about [*practice name*]?

2 What would you say the 'values' of [*practice name*] are?

3 What is it not so good at [*practice name*] and why?

4 If there were three things about [*practice name*] you could change, what would they be?

5 How well do you think [*practice name*] is managed?

6 Which of these apply to [*practice name*]?

	Strongly agree	Agree	Disagree	Strongly disagree	Don't know
The practice has a positive culture					
The senior management team work well together					
There is a clear business plan for the practice's development					
I understand the practice's business plan and my part in it					
Communication between management and staff is good					
Communication between departments is good					
Communication between offices is good					
The senior management team are highly motivated					
Fee earners are highly motivated					
Support staff are highly motivated					
The practice is well managed					
My skills are utilised to the full					

The practice is good at training and developing staff					
The practice's appraisal system works well					
The practice is good at marketing					
The practice is good at cross-selling					
The practice delivers high quality client care					
The practice is good at responding to enquiries from prospective clients					
The practice has a good reputation					
The practice makes good use of IT					
The practice's file management procedures are good					

7   What is [practice name]'s current reputation? How do you think clients or professional contacts would describe [practice name]?

8   What is your vision of [practice name] in five years' time? What should we be aiming for in terms of markets, reputation and profile?

9   Are there any practices which you consider are good role models for [practice name] to emulate?

Project plan template

[*Project name*]

Author			
Approver		**Date approved**	
Reviewer(s)			
Date created		**Plan version**	
Status		**Last updated**	

Document control

Version	Revised by	Date	Comments

1. Background

[*Insert overview*]

2. Objective

[*Insert objectives*]

3. Key performance indicators (KPIs)

Owner	Description	Rating	Key action(s)	Key date

4. Project scope

In	Out

5. Resources

Budget	
Human resources	
Technological	

6. Risks

Type	Description	Rating	Owner

7. Key milestones

Item	Due date	Owner	Comments

8. Recommendations

Description	Priority	[Unit/department/team]	Owner

APPENDIX 3A

Key performance indicators

Key performance indicators (KPIs) are measures of performance; as such, they need to be measurable. They should reflect the factors that are essential to, and will drive and underpin, the achievement of your objectives. For example, (a) management development and change, and (b) employees noticing the change and increasing productivity, may be drivers to the outcome of (c) increased sales.

The following are examples of KPIs in specific areas.

Customers:

- Customer satisfaction rates
- Time taken to answer telephone calls
- Percentage of events rated as 'excellent'
- Number of complaints
- Time taken to answer complaints
- Average time taken to fulfil customer orders/requests for information
- Response rates to advertisements or marketing activities
- Conversion rates
- Percentage of potential market acquired
- Number of new customers acquired

Employees:

- Absenteeism rates
- Employee turnover rates
- Time taken to process applications
- Percentage of employees promoted
- Percentage of appraisals completed on time
- Number of hours per year of career and skills development/training per employee
- Percentage of employees with development plans
- Satisfaction scores from the business on suitability/outcomes from training and development events

Financial:

- Percentage profit margins, sales, income
- Return on investment
- Percentage variation from budget
- Percentage of errors in payroll
- Percentage of expense claims processed within X days

- Time taken to prepare/issue invoices
- Credit turnaround time
- Average number of days from receipt of invoice to processing
- Percentage of errors in sales forecasts

Processes:

- Proportion of audits performed on schedule
- Percentage of reports published on schedule
- Percentage of project plans that meet schedule, price and quality
- Percentage of projects achieving desired outcomes
- Percentage of projects achieving key milestones
- Percentage of projects where expected benefits are realised
- Number of revisions to project plans
- Number of revisions to programme/project objectives
- Response time on requests for legal opinion
- Time taken to identify and resolve IT problems
- Number of security violations per year
- Percentage of departments with disaster recovery plans
- Percentage of 'downtime' on IT systems
- User satisfaction rates
- Number of visits to websites
- Number of pages of materials viewed over the Internet
- Cost of processing per invoice/application/payroll change, etc.

Targets

KPIs need to be quantifiable and measurable so that a target can be set – the expected level of performance that is being aimed for. Typically, targets are expressed in the following ways:

- Increase customer satisfaction rates by x% compared with 201X rates.
- At least x% of customers rate the service received as 'satisfactory' or 'very satisfactory'.
- Achieve £x increase on book sales compared with 201X sales.
- Improve net profit margin by x% compared with 201X margin.
- Reduce average cost of processing job applications to £x per application.
- Increase solicitors' awareness of the [specify] issue by x% from 201X baseline of x%.
- Increase average conversion rates for direct marketing activities from x% to x%.
- Reduce employee turnover rates from 201X baseline of x% to x%.
- Reduce downtime of business-critical systems to no more than x% by end of quarter 3.
- Achieve 'satisfactory rating' on file audits in at least x% of files.
- Improve return on investment by at least x% by end of quarter 2 and maintain at this rate or above for the remainder of the year.
- Implement a new performance management scheme by end of quarter 3.

- x% of managers complete appraisals on time.
- Reduce the average cost of recruitment by x%.
- x% of requests for information are responded to within x hours.
- x% of users rate member facilities as 'good' or 'very good'.

Mechanisms for measuring success

For each KPI, you will need to consider how you will measure and track performance and progress. If no suitable measurement systems already exist, you may need to create one. Typical mechanisms for measuring performance include:

- Customer/user satisfaction surveys and polls
- End of project reviews
- Data held on financial management system
- Data held on employee databases
- Data held on customer databases

When selecting your KPIs, take the following into account:

- Be clear about your desired outcome.
- Ensure suitability and consider cost.
- Consider the advantages and disadvantages of setting ambitious versus readily achievable targets.
- Be aware of value for money.

Below are 10 tests of a good measure:

1. The truth test – are you measuring what you set out to measure?
2. The focus test – are you only measuring what you set out to measure?
3. The relevance test – are you definitely measuring the right thing?
4. The consistency test – can/will the measurement be consistently taken?
5. The access test – can the data be easily accessed and understood?
6. The clarity test – is the measure clearly specified? Is there any ambiguity?
7. The so-what test – will the data be acted upon?
8. The timeliness test – is the data measured and acted upon in a timely fashion?
9. The cost test – is the measure worth the cost of capturing the data?
10. The gaming test – will the measure encourage undesirable behaviours?

APPENDIX 3B

Questions to consider in business planning

Where are we starting from?

- What services do we provide now, to whom and to what standard?
- Where do we get new clients from? Do we obtain recommendations from any particular sources?
- How are we viewed externally? What is outstanding? Are there any opportunities open to us to develop our skills and client base?
- What are our current strengths and weaknesses?
- Are there any areas of specialisation that could be developed further?
- What are the main threats facing us at the moment? How should we respond to these?
- How can we improve our (a) productivity; (b) efficiency; (c) client service; (d) profitability; (e) job and professional satisfaction; (f) management?

The next 3–5 years?

- What external changes are occurring that could impact on us? What strategies do we need to deal with them?
- What market sectors should we concentrate on?
- What should be our range of services?
- What should be our areas of specialisation in the longer term?
- What new services do we need to develop?

Where do we want to be?

- What is our target market position in five years' time?
- In three years' time?
- In 12 months' time?

Action plan

- Provide in detail on a quarterly basis for the next 12 months.
- Provide in outline for the subsequent two years.

APPENDIX 3C

Marketing plan template

Marketing plan [*year*]

Contents

1   Introduction

[*Outline of marketing plan*]

2   Branding

Market awareness

[*Overview*]

Existing users

[*Overview of those using visual identity*]

3   Target audiences

[*Overview of target audiences for marketing campaigns*]

4   Audience segmentation

[*Overview of target audience segments*]

Decision makers

Definition: [*outline of person with decision-making authority in target organisation*]

Group	Target	Decision maker	Influencers	Benefit

Influencers

Definition: [*outline of person/people who can influence the decision maker*]

Group	Target	Decision maker	Influencers	Benefit

Early adopters

Definition: [*outline of person/people who is/are likely to adopt product or service more quickly than others in target organisation*]

Group	Target	Decision maker	Influencers	Benefit

5   Market propositions

Tier 1

[*Details of highest level propositions*]

Tier 2

[Details of second highest level propositions]

6   Activities

Events

Title	Audience figure target	Focus	Budget	Occurrence

Direct mail

Title	Audience figure target	Focus	Budget	Occurrence

Public relations

Publication	Audience figure target	Message	Budget	Occurrence

Advertising

Publication	Audience figure target	Message	Budget	Occurrence

Website

[Outline]

7   Key milestones

Title	Description	Owner	Timescale

8   Recommendations

[Recommendation title]

[Outline]

APPENDIX 3D

Equality and diversity statements

Examples of statements are below:

- [*Name of practice*] is fully committed to equality and diversity in all of its functions. [*Name of practice*] believes that everyone has a right to be treated with dignity and respect and seeks to ensure that the principles of fairness and equality of opportunity for all underpin all its policies, plans, procedures, processes and practices. Please contact us if you would like a copy of our equality and diversity policy via: [*insert contact details*].

OR

- [*Name of practice*] is committed to promoting equality and diversity in all its dealings with clients, third parties and employees. Please contact us if you would like a copy of our equality and diversity policy via: [*insert contact details*].

OR

- [*Name of practice*] aims to be an inclusive employer and will select staff solely on merit, irrespective of race, sex, disability, age, religion and faith, or sexual orientation. In order to monitor the effectiveness of our equality and diversity policy, we request all applicants to provide us the information asked for on the job application form. A copy of the policy is available on request via: [*insert contact details*].

OR

- [*Name of practice*] aims to promote equality of opportunity in employment, in its dealing with clients and in service delivery, and has a policy for this purpose. The policy covers all aspects of employment, from advertising vacancies, recruitment and selection, training and conditions of service, and all aspects of professional dealings with clients, including the engagement of professional services. A copy of the policy is available on request via: [*insert contact details*].

An introduction to the Equality Impact Assessment process

What is an EIA?

An Equality Impact Assessment (EIA) is a thorough, detailed and systematic analysis of the potential or actual effects of an activity (policy, criteria, practice or function). It is carried out to determine whether the activity has an impact (either positive or negative) on a particular group of people, for example, in terms of age (older or younger people), gender, disability, race, sexual orientation, or religion or belief.

What needs an EIA?

EIAs are recommended for all of our existing and new activities. This includes unwritten policies and procedures and informal decisions. Remember, just because something we do is not written down in a document does not mean it has no impact, and to follow best practice we should assess it. This requirement extends to the assessment of our internal and external websites and communications for both our staff and clients.

What is the purpose of an EIA?

Our policies, procedures, functions and decisions affect people differently. EIAs help us to see how policies, practices or products/services can potentially or actually impact on different groups. This includes being able to identify and demonstrate the positive effects as well as any potential or actual adverse effects.

EIAs help us to ensure that we do not unlawfully disadvantage people and that we are fair and inclusive in everything that we do. They also help us to ensure that we have considered the needs, circumstances and concerns of those who are/will be affected by our decisions/service delivery.

When should we carry out an EIA?

We should conduct EIAs:

- on all our existing key activities;
- when we are developing a new activity;
- when we are presenting a proposal or policy to decision makers;
- if evidence, concerns or issues come to light regarding accessibility and barriers to our service.

What's involved in carrying out an EIA?

There are two main stages to an EIA:

- initial assessment; and
- full assessment.

Additional information about EIAs, including a template EIA report, can be requested via: **www.lawsociety.org.uk/inclusioncharter** or e-mail: **inclusioncharter@ lawsociety.org.uk**.

See also **www.lawsociety.org.uk/cpdcentre** and page ii for details of the Law Society's online training package *Equality and Diversity in Practice*.